Hanon

Piano / Keyboard

Exercises 1 - 30

Condensed and Simplified for

Beginners Easy Reading

Martin Woodward

ISBN: 978-1-326-17051-6

Enquires: http://gonkmusic.com

Acknowledgements

To all the fantastic musicians who I've had the privilege of working with back in the 1960s / 70s including: Pip Williams (guitarist / record producer); Tex Marsh (drums); Roger Flavell (bassist / singer / songwriter); Kevan Fogarty (guitarist); Ralph Denyer (singer / songwriter); Phil Childs (bassist); Jim Smith (drums); George Lee (saxophonist); Ron Thomas (bassist); Emile Ford (UK No. 1 singer / songwriter).

To my early mentors: Alan Simonds (guitarist / vocalist); big bruv Steve (guitarist) and Mr. Henley (my inspirational music teacher at Warlingham School 1960 - 65).

And to Myriad Software: http://www.myriad-online.com for the Harmony Assistant music notation software which was used to produce this book. - *Thanks!*

Contents

Introduction

In this short book you will find condensed and simplified versions of the Hanon piano finger exercises 1 - 30 as well as the major, harmonic minor and melodic minor scales in every key (two octaves).

What is Hanon?

The *'Hanon Virtuoso Pianist'* is a collection of piano finger exercises designed to give equal strength, agility and flexibility to all five fingers of both hands. Written by Charles-Louis Hanon in the 1800s, these exercises without doubt have become one of the most widely used techniques by today's pianists. In my opinion these are the best finger exercises available.

One really great thing about these exercises is that they are applicable to both absolute beginners and advanced players alike, particularly as the reading ability required is minimal. Whatever your ability, these exercises will help improve your technique and finger strength.

Having been written well over 100 years ago, the original work is now in the public domain and therefore digital copies can be acquired free of charge on the internet. However, most of these are very poor quality and the instructions are mainly in French or Russian - *neither of which work too well for me!* For the full version I personally recommend the *'Alfred'* Edition edited by Allan Small which is clear and has instructions in English.

So why do I need this book?

The whole point is to make it easy to read and to reduce page turns - *less is more!* In the full version the first 30 exercises take up fifty pages whereas here there are three exercises per page for the first 20, then two per page for the next 10, reducing the fifty pages to just twelve. I initially produced this for my own use only but figured that others may like to take advantage of what I've done.

Does this mean that the print is just smaller?

No, not at all. If you are familiar with these exercises, you will know that they are repeated patterns which ascend and descend for two octaves diatonically.

To condense and simplify them and consequently eliminate an enormous amount of page turns I have shown:

- the all-important fingering on the first pattern (as per the original)

- then the repeated second pattern

- then *'changeover'* patterns between ascending and descending - which are sometimes slightly different

---

- then finally the last pattern of each exercise which again is often very slightly different.

I have also written them two octaves apart (for easy reading) and only shown them for one octave instead of two. In practice they should be played one octave apart and ultimately be practiced for two octaves.

You can print out any or all the pages as required (the link for the pdf printable version is given at the end of the book).

For those not familiar with the basic format, I have included the first exercise in full as written in the original version (well I've written this in **4/4** and quavers rather than **2/4** and semi-quavers). If you compare this with the first simplified and condensed exercise you should see exactly what I have done and hopefully why!

What do you mean by 'diatonically'?

All the exercises are in the scale of **C major**, and as the patterns ascend and descend, they continue to use the notes of the scale rather than transposing.

So, are you suggesting that I miss out the missing sections?

No, no, no, the idea is that you play the complete exercises as written in the first full example, but you will need to play the missing sections *without* the music notation except for the changeover patterns (between ascending and descending) and the end patterns.

But what if I can only play by reading music?

Of course, sight reading music is a good idea, but these exercises are not *'reading'* exercises, they are simply repeated patterns to improve finger technique. This is easy without reading the music as the patterns simply move up and down with the scale notes. In fact, you don't even need to know any scales as each pattern simply uses the next white note up from the previous when ascending and the next white note down when descending, using the same pattern and fingering as shown. For instance, if the first ascending pattern starts on **'C'**, the next pattern will start on **'D'** then **'E'** etc. In short - if you can play the first pattern (as written) you can play the rest! All the fingering needed is shown in the patterns written.

Instructions for use

Ideally use a metronome and begin as slowly as you need to gradually increase speed according to your ability. The tempo guidelines in the original are 60 bpm - 108 bpm, BUT the original is written in semi-quavers whereas the first 20 exercises here are written in quavers, so the metronome speed should be doubled (120 - 216). Exercises 21 - 30 are written in semi-quavers here as per the original. There is no point in increasing the speed beyond your capability. If you practice regularly, speed will come on its own!

In all cases your hands should be in a claw like position, lift the fingers high and play each note with equal velocity. Learn and practice each exercise in strict numerical rotation as they are arranged to give rest to the fingers where fatigue has been caused previously.

Make sure that you are thoroughly familiar with the first 20 exercises before proceeding further. Take your time, there's no rush - *unless you want to be a concert pianist next week, in which case good luck!*

* Notice the difference in patterns in Ex 12. The first pattern starts with a fifth interval whereas the second and subsequent patterns start with a sixth interval. This occurs again at the end of the descent. I have emphasised this with asterisks in the notation.

Navigation

If using the digital version, you can revert to the *'Contents'* with a single click, by using the « icon found in the footer of every page. Then you can navigate to any exercise by clicking your choice in the *'Contents'*.

There are also a few other internal hyperlinks which are underlined where available.

Audio Files

In the digital pdf version all of the Hanon exercises can be heard by clicking on the notation for each exercise, as can the first major and minor scales. While you do this, you will lose the page view, but you should be able to revert back to this while the audio is playing so that you can see each exercise at the same time as listening to it.

Please download the pdf version from the link at the end of the book. to hear these (they may not work in the Kindle version). Alternatively, all the audio files can be heard at https://learn-keyboard.co.uk/audio-links/hanon.html.

Hanon Exercise 1 - as written

1.

Ascending

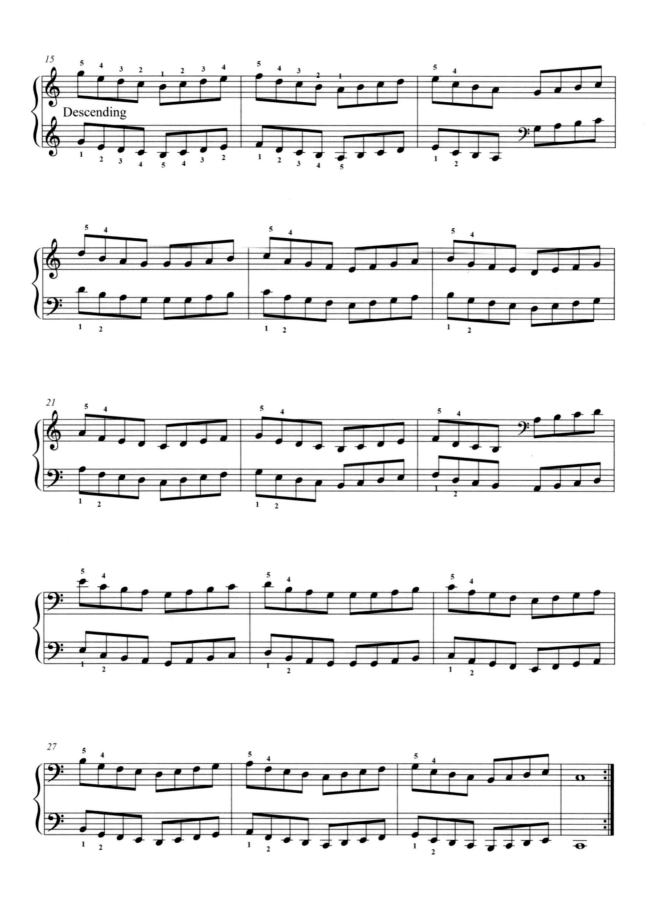

Hanon Exercises 1 - 2 - 3

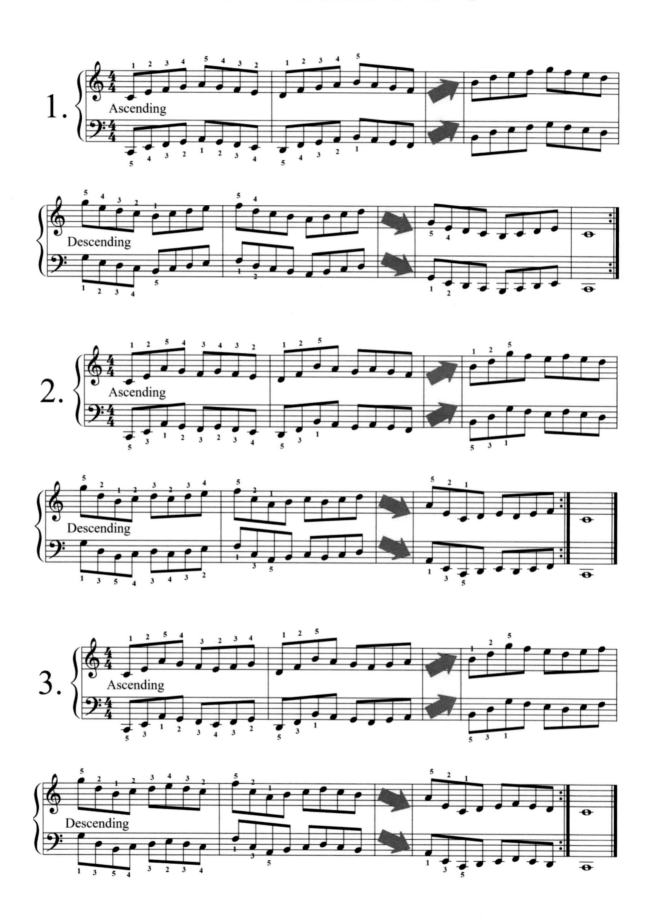

Hanon Exercises 4 - 5 - 6

Hanon Exercises 7 - 8 - 9

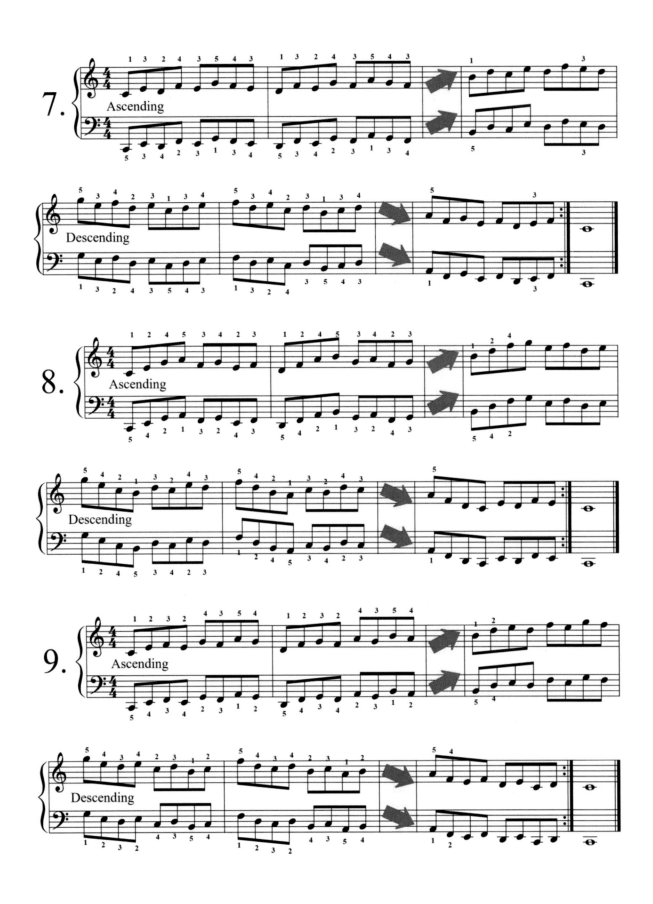

Hanon Exercises 10 - 11 - 12

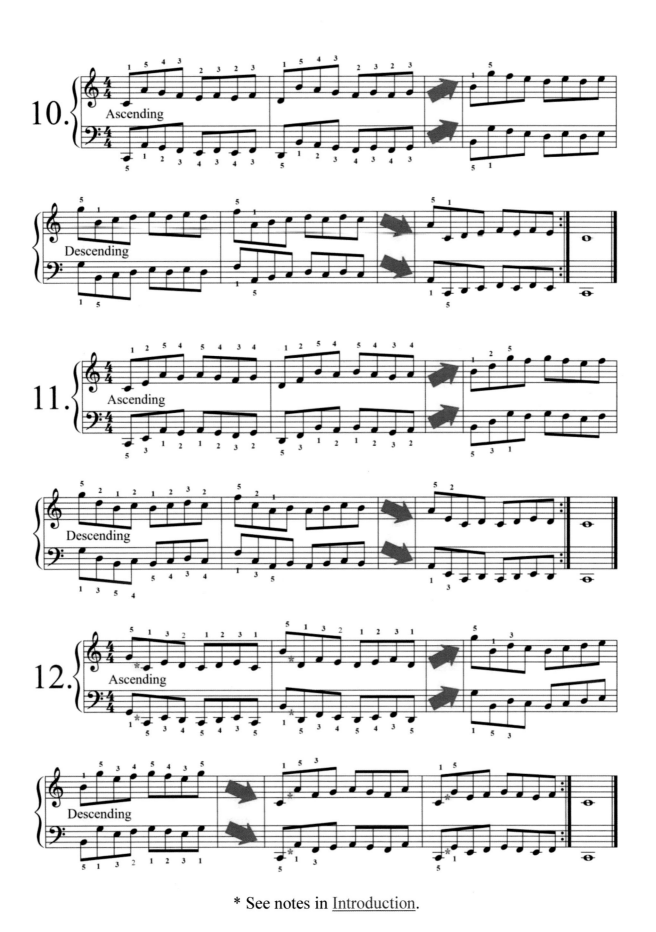

* See notes in Introduction.

Hanon Exercises 13 - 14 - 15

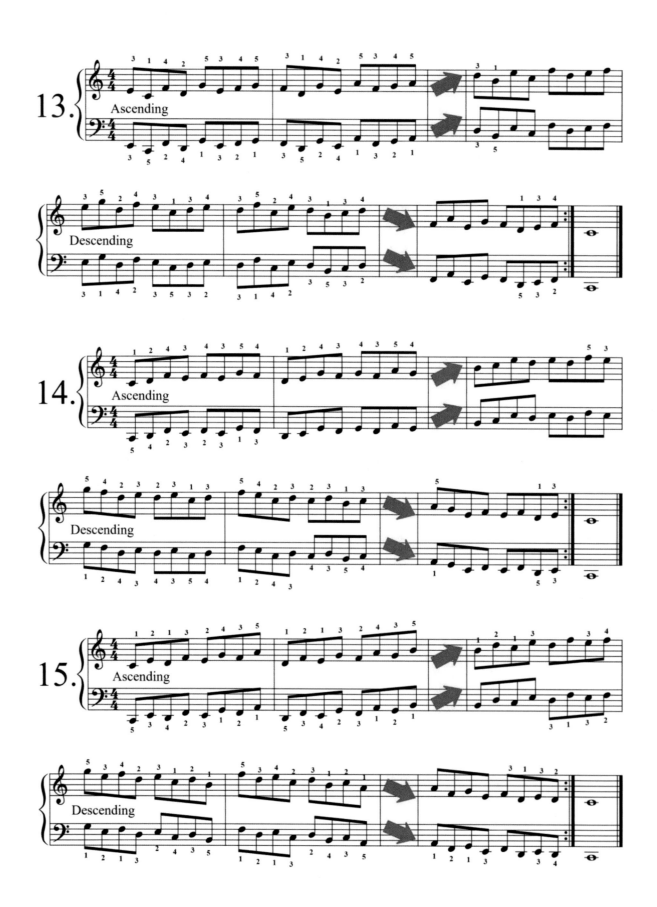

Hanon Exercises 16 - 17 - 18

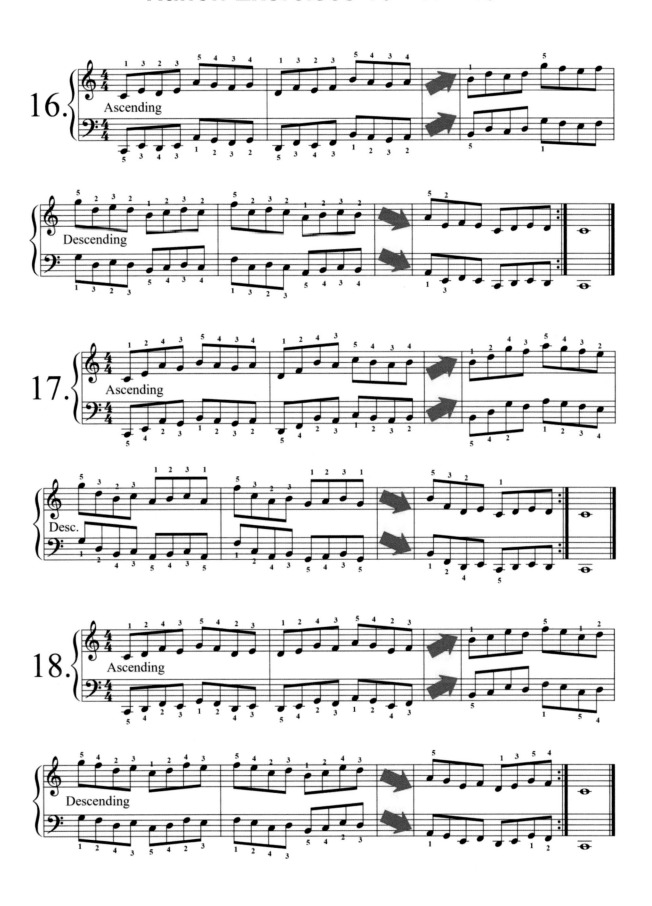

Hanon Exercises 19 - 20

Hanon Exercises 21 - 22

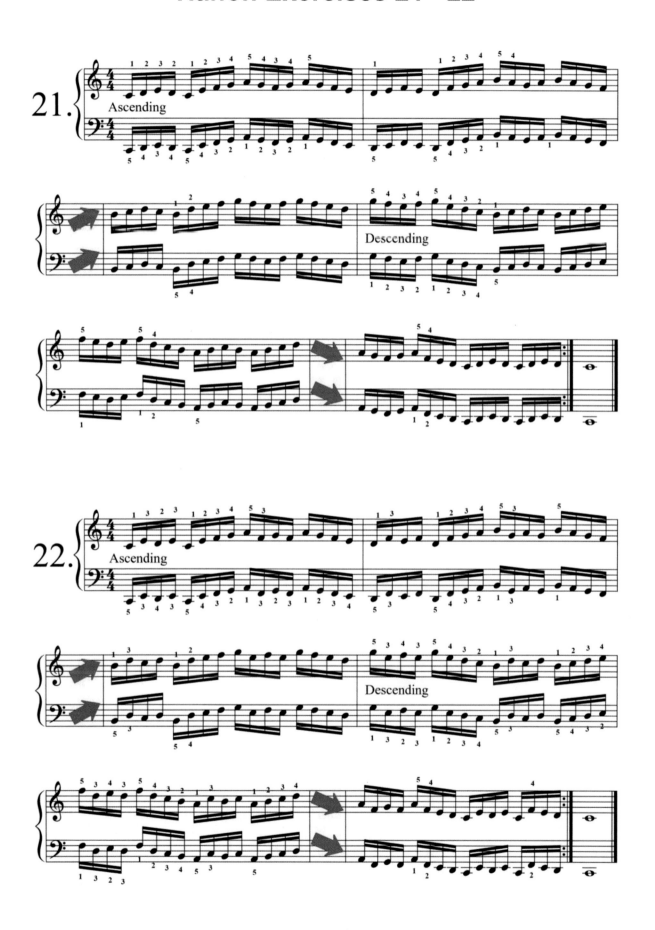

Hanon Exercises 23 - 24

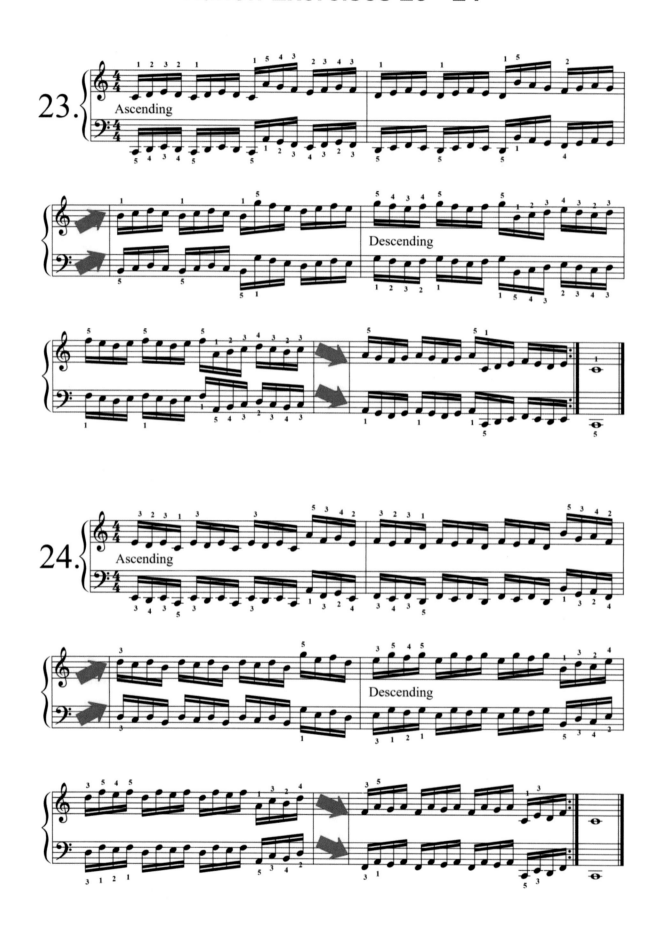

Hanon Exercises 25 - 26

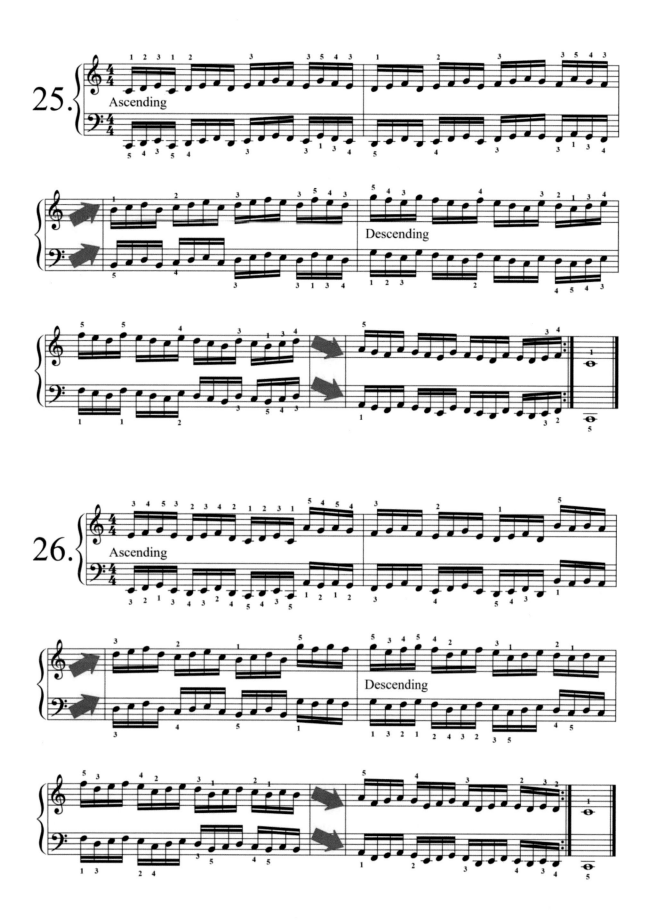

Hanon Exercises 27 - 28

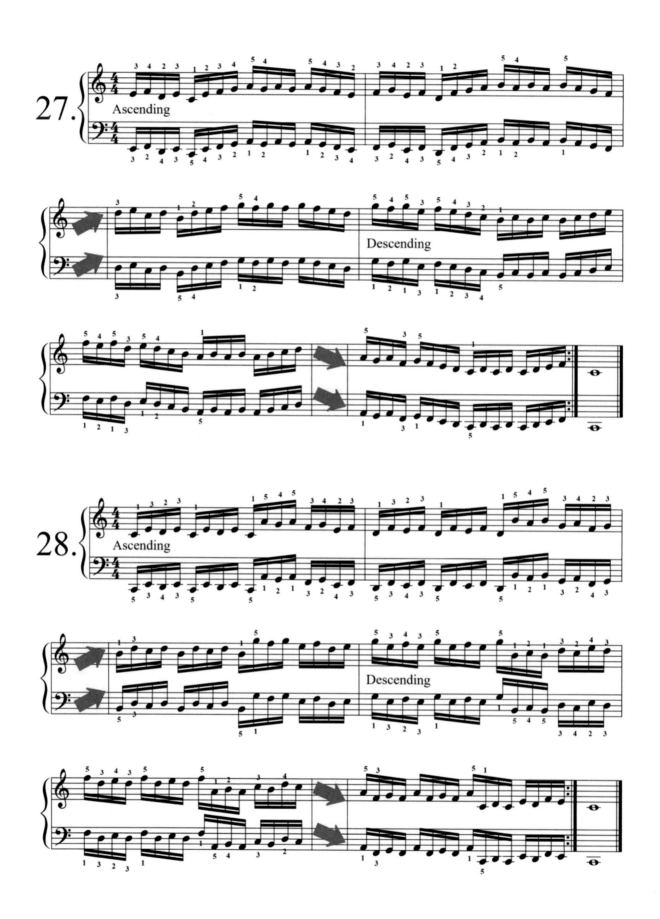

Hanon Exercises 29 – 30

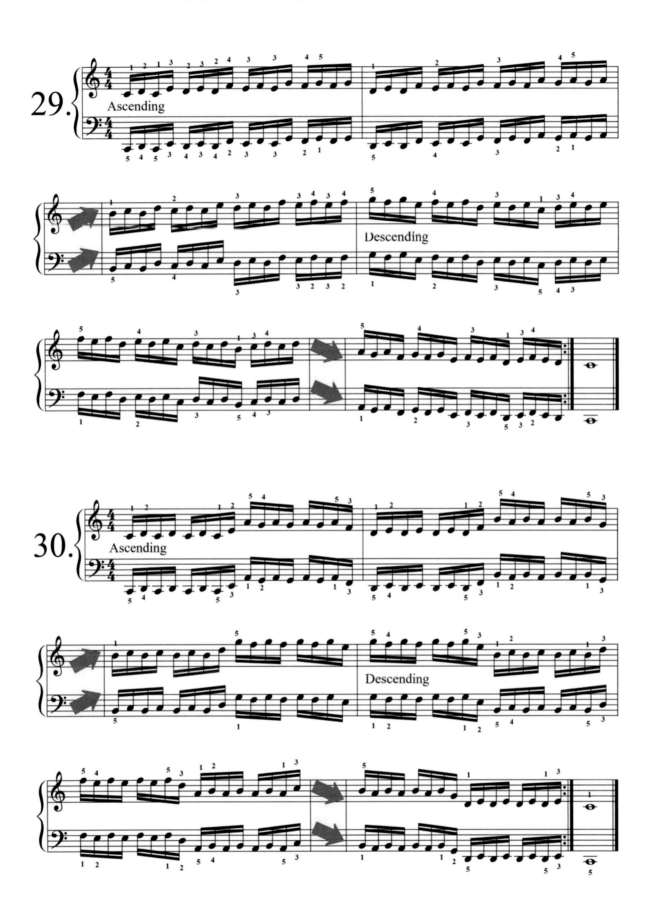

Scale Exercises major / minor

The next few pages show all the major and relative minor scales in the order in which they should be learnt. They are written here in two octaves, one octave apart, but can also be played for three or four octaves. Ideally these should be practiced with each hand separately and both hands together staccato and legato paying attention to accuracy and timing. Also make sure that each note is played with an equal pressure. Gradually increase the speed according to your ability. When you are familiar with them, they can be practiced in any order.

If you have the eBook version, you can of course print out the pages that you require. Or if you have the printed version, you can download the digital version in order to hear the examples of the **C major** / **A minor** scales by clicking on the notation.

Note that the fingering is identical for every scale starting on a white note except for **F major** and both of the **F minors** where the *right hand* uses the 4th finger on **B flat**, and **B major** and both of the **B minors** where the *left hand* starts with the 4th finger on the tonic (**B**).

There are significant fingering variations to all the scales starting on black notes for both hands. In all cases make a special note of where the 4th finger goes!

Also note that the fingering for **F#** and **C# melodic minors** is different *ascending* and *descending* in the *right hand*, as is the **G# melodic minor** in the *left hand*.

C major Scale

A Harmonic Minor Scale

A Melodic Minor Scale

F major Scale

D Harmonic Minor Scale

D Melodic Minor Scale

G major Scale

E Harmonic Minor Scale

E Melodic Minor Scale

23

D Major Scale

B Harmonic Minor Scale

B Melodic Minor Scale

B♭ Major Scales

G Harmonic Minor Scale

G Melodic Minor Scale

E♭ Major Scales

C Harmonic Minor Scale

C Melodic Minor Scale

A Major Scales

F# Harmonic Minor Scale

F# Melodic Minor Scale

E Major Scales

C# Harmonic Minor Scale

C# Melodic Minor Scale

A♭ Major Scales

F Harmonic Minor Scale

F Melodic Minor Scale

B Major Scales

G# Harmonic Minor Scale

G# Melodic Minor Scale

D♭ Major Scales

B♭ Harmonic Minor Scale

B♭ Melodic Minor Scale

Gb Major Scales

Eb Harmonic Minor Scale

Eb Melodic Minor Scale

Thank You

Well, that's it folks, but finally and most importantly, I'd like to thank you kindly for buying this book. It's been my sincere desire to give excellent value for money with this and all my books. I've worked very long and very hard to achieve this and hope that you think I've succeeded.

If you've enjoyed this, your positive feedback (on Google / Amazon / Lulu etc.) would be very much appreciated. - *Thanks!*

Please feel free to contact me at https://learn-keyboard.co.uk/contact_us.html if you have any queries. I'd be pleased to hear from you, and I will always answer (unless I've snuffed it), but please check your spam box just in case my reply goes amiss.

Download link

If you have the paperback or kindle version, you can download the pdf (printable) version without further cost here: https://learn-keyboard.co.uk/hanon_dl.html (note the underscore between hanon and dl), but please honour my copyright and the hard work I've put into this by using this for your own use only. Thank you!

Further Reading

You may also perhaps be interested in some of the following books, the details for which can all be seen on my websites at https://learn-keyboard.co.uk and http://gonkmusic.com.

If copying the links be sure to include the hyphen in *'learn-keyboard'*.

Made in the USA
Middletown, DE
26 September 2023

39463021R00022